## Science Matters
# EARTHQUAKES

### Jennifer Nault

**WEIGL PUBLISHERS INC.**

**Published by Weigl Publishers Inc.**
350 5th Avenue, Suite 3304, PMB 6G
New York, NY USA 10118-0069
Web site: www.weigl.com
Copyright 2005 WEIGL PUBLISHERS INC.

**Library of Congress Cataloging-in-Publication Data**

Nault, Jennifer.
   Earthquakes / Jennifer Nault.
      p. cm. -- (Science matters)
   Includes index.
   ISBN 1-59036-212-8 (lib. bdg. : alk. paper)  ISBN 1-59036-248-9 (softcover)
   1.  Earthquakes--Juvenile literature.  I. Title. II. Series.
   QE521.3.N38 2005
   551.22--dc22

                                    2004004134

Printed in the United States of America
1 2 3 4 5 6 7 8 9 0  08 07 06 05 04

              **Project Coordinator** Tina Schwartzenberger  **Copy Editor** Frances Purslow
                          **Design** Terry Paulhus  **Layout** Bryan Pezzi
                              **Photo Researcher** Ellen Bryan

**Photograph Credits**

Every reasonable effort has been made to trace ownership and to obtain permission to reprint copyright material. The publishers would be pleased to have any errors or omissions brought to their attention so that they may be corrected in subsequent printings.

**Cover:** Izmit (Kocaeli), Turkey, earthquake from National Information Service for Earthquake Engineering, University of California, Berkeley
**Lloyd Cluff/CORBIS/MAGMA:** page 6; **Corel Corporation:** page 10; **Bruce Leighty:** page 15; **National Archives and Records Administration—Pacific Region, San Bruno, California:** page 14; **Courtesy National Information Service for Earthquake Engineering, University of California, Berkeley:** page 7; **Bryan Pezzi:** pages 12-13; **Photos.com:** pages 3T, 3M, 3B, 17, 19, 21, 22T, 22B, 23T, 23B; **United States Geological Survey:** pages 1 (J.K. Nakata), 4 (C.E. Meyer), 8 (C.E. Meyer); **Visuals Unlimited:** pages 16 (Inga Spence), 18 (Inga Spence).

# Contents

# Studying Earthquakes

Shaking or trembling of the ground is an earthquake. Earthquakes occur when rocks along a crack in Earth's surface suddenly shift. The earthquake releases stress that has slowly built up in the rocks.

Most earthquakes are too small for people to feel. Some earthquakes are bigger. A few cause great damage. Earthquakes have killed thousands of people. Earthquakes can cause buildings to fall, roads to crack, and water dams to burst.

● During an earthquake, bricks and other falling objects can cause damage and injuries.

# Earthquake Facts

**Scientists think that more than one million earthquakes occur each year. Only 100 of these cause damage. Keep reading to learn more facts about earthquakes.**

- Earthquakes cannot be prevented. Scientists study earthquakes. They **predict** where future earthquakes may occur.

- Earthquakes can leave long cracks in the ground. It can appear as though the ground has split in two.

- The energy released from a big earthquake is enormous. It is the same as millions of explosives being set off at the same time.

- People did not understand how earthquakes happened until the early twentieth century.

# Earth on the Move

Earth's surface is always moving. Earth's **crust** is broken into tectonic plates. These are large pieces of crust that shift and move. They are always joining together and pulling apart. When tectonic plates move, the edges grate or scrape against each other. This movement causes Earth to tremble. The place where tectonic plates meet is called a fault line.

● Fault lines can be one inch or many miles long. They may also be vertical, horizontal, or slanted at any angle.

# Birth of an Earthquake

When tectonic plates rub against each other, they create pressure. Over time, the pressure builds. The pressure may build over many years. When the pressure grows too strong, the plates suddenly move. The pressure is let go. **Shock waves** move through Earth's crust. Shock waves cause the ground to shake and tremble. This is an earthquake.

Most earthquakes in the United States take place in Alaska. As many as 4,000 are recorded in Alaska each year.

# Earthquakes in Focus

Earthquakes begin deep underground. The place where energy is first released is called the focus. The focus can be near Earth's surface. The closer the focus is to the surface, the more damage the earthquake will cause.

The earthquake begins on Earth's surface above the focus. This spot is called the epicenter. Here, the shock waves are strongest. The epicenter is usually where the most damage occurs.

● An earthquake occurs somewhere in the world every 30 seconds. Most are too small to cause any damage.

# Earthquake Scale

**Some earthquakes are very powerful. Others can hardly be felt.**

Dr. Charles Richter created a way to measure earthquakes in 1935. The Richter scale measures the height of **seismic** waves. The scale gives number values to the amount of energy created during an earthquake. The number linked to an earthquake is called its **magnitude**.

| MAGNITUDE | EFFECT |
| --- | --- |
| 1 | Cannot be felt on the surface |
| 2 | Can only be felt slightly near the epicenter |
| 3 | Can be felt near the epicenter, but causes little damage |
| 4–5 | Can cause damage in small areas and is felt about 20 miles (32 kilometers) away |
| 6 | Can be felt over a large area and can cause much more damage |
| 7 | Can cause buildings to fall and people to die |
| 8 | Widespread **destruction** |

# Earthquake Areas

Earthquakes can happen at any time. They can strike anywhere in the world. Most earthquakes happen along the edges of tectonic plates. Usually, this is near the edges of **continents**.

There are two main areas where earthquakes occur. One is called the circum-Pacific belt. It circles the Pacific Ocean. This area includes the western coasts of Japan, North and South America, and the Philippines. The other area is called the Alpide belt. It cuts through Europe and Asia.

• Ten percent of all earthquakes occur in Japan. Japan experiences the most earthquakes in the world.

# Earthquakes Around the World

**Earthquakes have caused great damage around the world. Below are details about some of the worst earthquakes in history.**

## ARMENIA

An earthquake of 6.9 on the Richter scale shook Armenia in 1988. Between 25,000 and 100,000 people were killed. Almost all of the buildings fell in some towns. People were not prepared. Most did not have rescue plans.

## JAPAN

In 1923, the Great Kanto Earthquake shook Japan. It measured 8.3 on the Richter scale. More than 100,000 people died. The earthquake's focus was under the sea. This caused a huge **tsunami**.

## CHILE

Santiago, Chile, had the strongest earthquake ever recorded. It happened in 1960. It measured 9.5 on the Richter scale. About 3,000 people were killed, and the beaches were washed away.

# Earthquakes Close-up

What does an earthquake look like from inside Earth? Scientists have studied earthquakes for many years. They have learned how an earthquake happens and what it looks like.

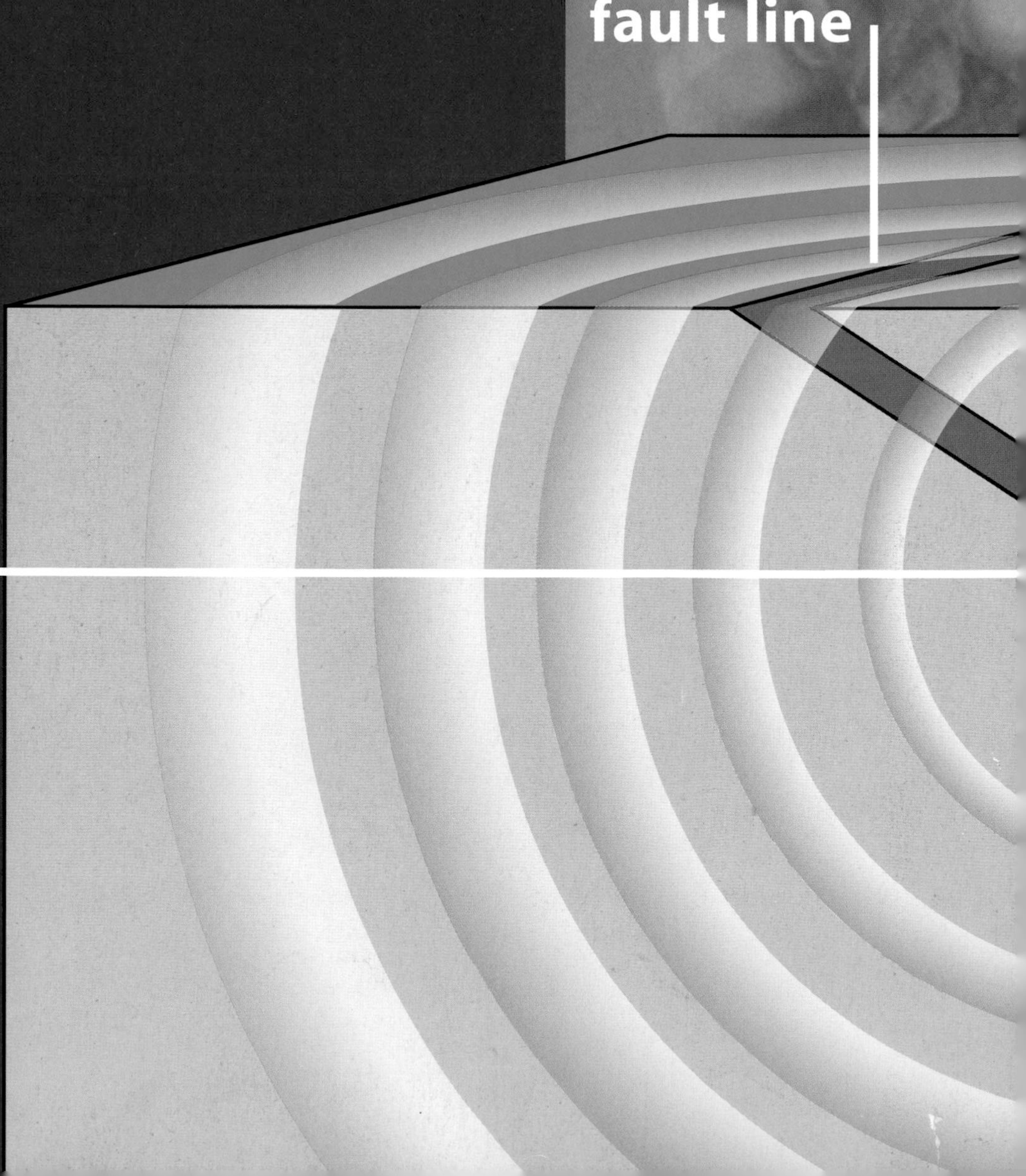

**fault line**

**focus**

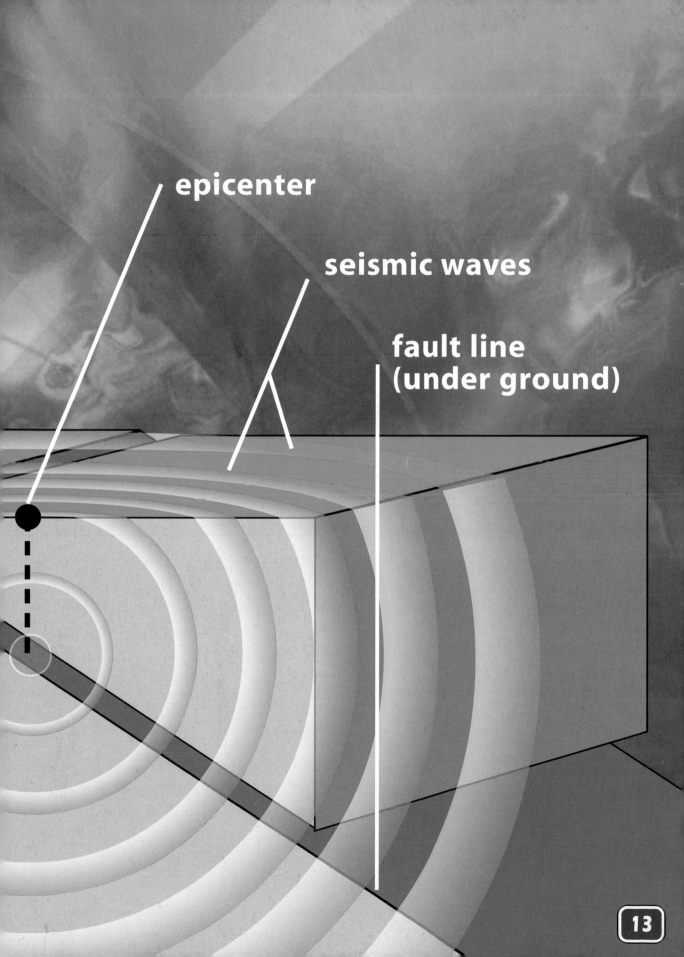

epicenter

seismic waves

fault line
(under ground)

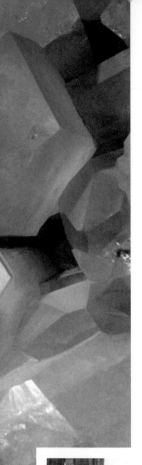

# All Shook Up

Many earthquakes shake the state of California. The San Andreas Fault is a large fault line. It runs more than 680 miles (1,100 km) through California. Many earthquakes happen along this fault line.

In 1906, a large earthquake struck San Francisco. It measured 8.3 on the Richter scale. Buildings crashed to the ground. Many people were killed. The earthquake also started a terrible fire, which burned through the city. The fire may have caused even more damage than the earthquake.

● In 1906, few of San Francisco's buildings were designed to withstand earthquakes.

# Living Near Earthquakes

Earthquakes cannot be stopped. People who live in earthquake areas can protect themselves. People can practice how to **evacuate** a building safely. They can learn where to find safe places to wait for an earthquake to stop. Standing in a doorway or sitting under a strong table is best.

Safer buildings will also protect people during earthquakes. Buildings that stand on solid rock are safer than those built on soft ground. Wooden buildings are also safer than brick or stone buildings. The Transamerica Building in San Francisco has a flexible **foundation**. It can sway back and forth during an earthquake without breaking apart or falling down.

# Earthquake Watchers

Some scientists study earthquakes. They research Earth's seismic activity. Seismologists look for the cause, kind, and size of seismic activity. They predict where earthquakes may occur. Seismologists work with special tools and computers to study earthquakes.

● There are more than 1,000 seismographic stations in the world.

# Tremor Time

Here is a fun experiment. You will learn how distance affects energy in Earth.

Find a small table. Be sure that nothing is on the table. At one end of the table, build a small square using 20 dominoes. Stand the dominoes on their edges. Put a piece of cardboard on top of your domino walls to make a roof. Go to the opposite end of the table and hit it with your hand. Your dominoes will probably shake but will not fall. Go back to the opposite end of the table. Hit this side of the table. What happened this time?

Your domino house probably fell down. When objects are close to shock waves, the energy has more effect on the objects. Shock waves have less effect on objects farther away from the shock waves.

# Measuring Movement

Seismologists use special instruments to measure changes in Earth. One tool is the seismograph. A seismograph measures and records vibrations on the ground and inside Earth. It produces wavy lines on paper. These lines record how Earth's crust is moving.

Computers are also useful tools to seismologists. Computers record and mimic Earth's movements. Rock movement can be measured using laser beams. Strainmeters measure tectonic plate activity. Strainmeters use laser beams to record the tiniest movements in Earth.

• Computerized seismographs allow seismologists to track earthquakes to within 6 miles (10 km) of the epicenter.

# Earthquake Myth

Cultures all over the world have earthquake myths. Hindus thought eight huge elephants held Earth up. Sometimes an elephant would grow tired. It would shake its head to wake up. This caused Earth to vibrate.

California's Gabrielino Native Peoples believed the Great Spirit created a beautiful place with lakes and rivers. Six large turtles carried this place on their backs. One day, the turtles began to fight. Three of the turtles swam east. At the same time, the others swam west. This caused Earth to vibrate and crack. The land on the turtles' backs was too heavy. They could not swim far. They stopped fighting.

Sometimes the turtles under California fight again. They cause Earth to shake.

# Surfing Our Earth

**How can I find more information about earthquakes?**
- Libraries have many interesting books about earthquakes.
- Science centers are great places to learn about earthquakes.
- The Internet offers some great Web sites dedicated to earthquakes.

**Where can I find a good reference Web site to learn more about earthquakes?**
Encarta Homepage
www.encarta.com
- Type any earthquake-related term into the search engine. Some terms to try include "tectonic plates" and "epicenter."

**How can I find out more about recent earthquakes and faults?**
U.S. Geological Survey Earthquake Hazards Program for Kids
http://earthquake.usgs.gov/4kids
- This Web site offers earthquake science projects, an earthquake glossary, and the latest news on earthquakes around the world.

# Science in Action

## Plan Ahead

It is always a good idea to have an earthquake plan. Think about where you spend the most time indoors. Is it in a classroom or somewhere in your home? From this location, where is the closest doorway? Where is the nearest strong table? These are both good places to wait for an earthquake to stop.

## Be a Seismograph

You can record a bumpy road just like a seismograph records Earth's movements.

You will need:
- car and driver
- felt pen
- pad of lined paper

Ask the driver to find a bumpy road. Put the pen in your hand and hold your arm straight out. Be sure to keep your arm stiff. With the other hand, place the pad of paper in front of the pen. You can lean the pad against the dashboard. Every time you hit a bump, the pen will move up and down on the paper. These marks are similar to a seismograph.

# What Have You Learned?

**1** Where do most earthquakes occur?

**2** What is the name of the scale that measures the level of an earthquake?

**3** Would a magnitude 3 earthquake cause terrible damage?

**4** What is the name for the place where tectonic plates meet?

**5** What is the focus?

**6** On Earth's surface, the shock waves are strongest at this place.

**7** What is the name of the fault line that runs through California?

**8** What kind of work do seismologists perform?

**9** What can laser beams measure?

**10** Which animals did the Gabrielino Native Peoples think held up the Earth?

Answers: 1. Along the edges of tectonic plates 2. The Richter scale 3. No 4. A fault line 5. The underground place where energy is first released during an earthquake 6. The epicenter 7. The San Andreas Fault 8. Seismologists research earthquakes. 9. Rock movement 10. Turtles

# Words to Know

**continents:** the seven main land masses of Earth—Africa, Antarctica, Asia, Australia, Europe, North America, and South America

**crust:** Earth's hard, top layer

**destruction:** great damage or ruin

**evacuate:** to leave a dangerous area

**foundation:** the base on which a building stands

**magnitude:** the size and strength of an earthquake

**mimic:** act like something else

**predict:** to say what may happen in the future

**seismic:** caused by an earthquake

**shock waves:** bursts of energy that come from the rocks in Earth's crust

**tsunami:** a powerful wave created when an earthquake occurs on the ocean floor

# Index